A

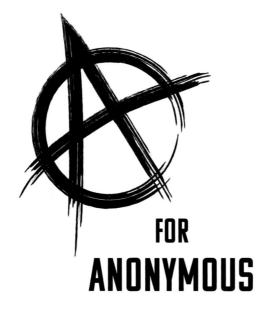

FOR

ANONYMOUS

FOR
ANONYMOUS

HOW A MYSTERIOUS HACKER COLLECTIVE
TRANSFORMED THE WORLD

DAVID KUSHNER

ILLUSTRATED BY KOREN SHADMI

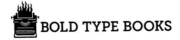
BOLD TYPE BOOKS

Bold Type Books
116 East 16th Street, 8th Floor New York, NY 10003
www.boldtypebooks.org
@BoldTypeBooks

Printed in the United States of America

First Edition: March 2020

Published by Bold Type Books, an imprint of Perseus Books, LLC, a subsidiary of Hachette Book Group, Inc. Bold Type Books is a co-publishing venture of the Type Media Center and Perseus Books.

The Hachette Speakers Bureau provides a wide range of authors for speaking events. To find out more, go to www.hachettespeakersbureau.com or call (866) 376-6591.

The publisher is not responsible for websites (or their content) that are not owned by the publisher.

Print book interior design by Koren Shadmi.

Library of Congress Control Number: 2019950854

ISBNs: 978-1-56858-878-0 (paperback), 978-1-56858-879-7 (paper over board), 978-1-56858-877-3 (ebook)

LSC-W

10 9 8 7 6 5 4 3 2 1

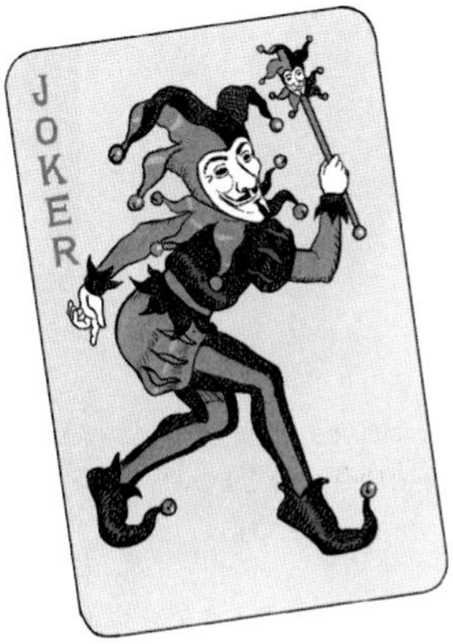
JOKER

CHAPTER 1

3B

NAME?

DELTA

DAVID KUSHNER.

NAME?

DAVID KUSHNER.

BUSINESS OR PLEASURE?

BUSINESS.

OH? WHAT DO YOU DO?

I'M A WRITER.

WHAT DO YOU WRITE?

WORKING ON AN ARTICLE FOR THE NEW YORKER.

COOL! DO YOU NEED A GPS?

I'M GOOD.

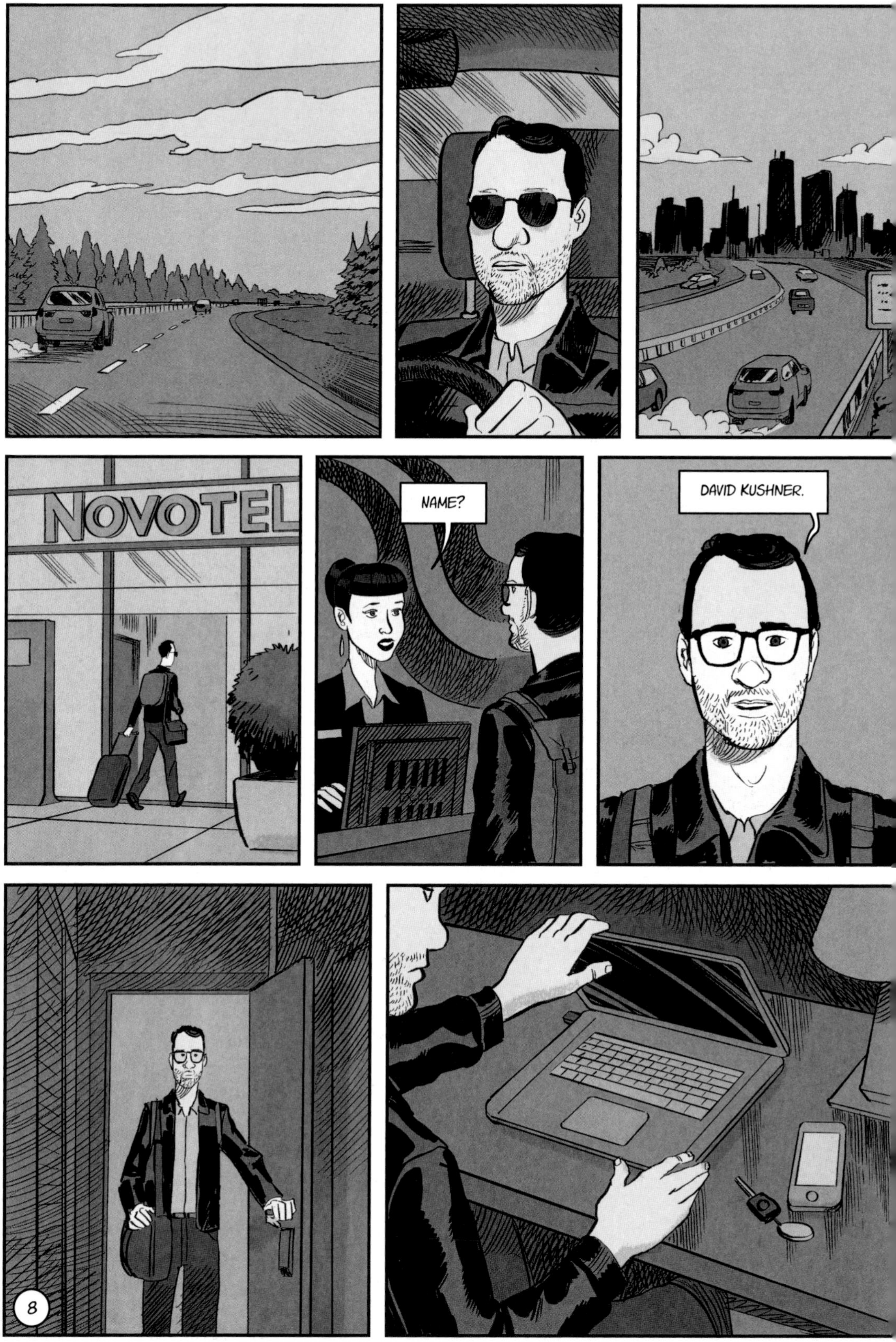
NOVOTEL
NAME?
DAVID KUSHNER.

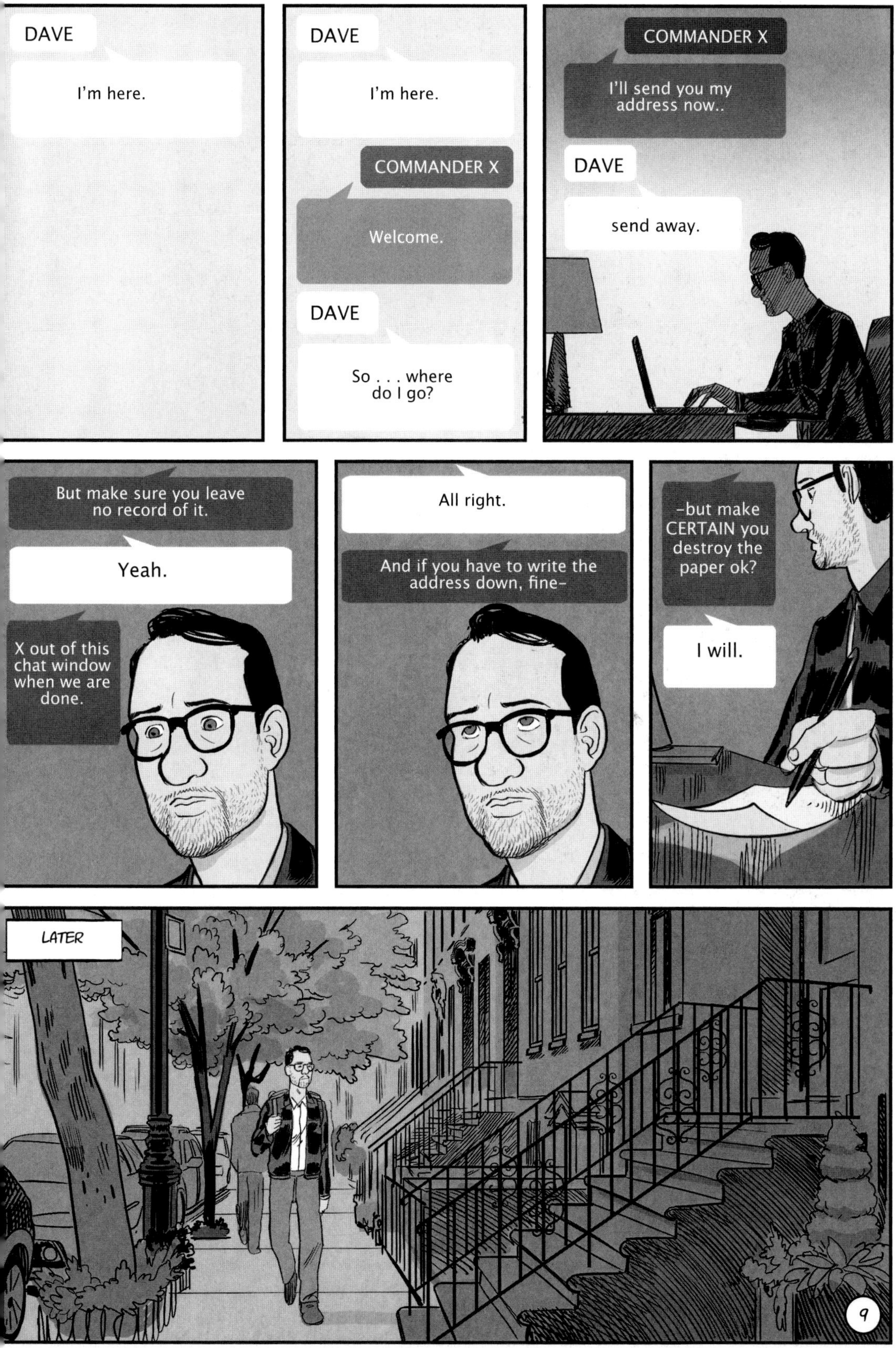
DAVE
I'm here.
DAVE
I'm here.
COMMANDER X
Welcome.
DAVE
So . . . where do I go?
COMMANDER X
I'll send you my address now..
DAVE
send away.
But make sure you leave no record of it.
Yeah.
X out of this chat window when we are done.
All right.
And if you have to write the address down, fine-
-but make CERTAIN you destroy the paper ok?
I will.
LATER

THIS MUST BE IT.

HEY, IT'S ME.

COME IN.

I HOPE YOU DON'T MIND THE SMOKE.

NAH, I'M FINE.

COFFEE?

SURE.

SO YOU MADE IT.

YEAH.

THE WAY of ZEN

ALAN WATTS

THOUGH IT WOULD HAVE BEEN EASIER JUST TO FLY STRAIGHT HERE INSTEAD OF DRIVING FOR THREE HOURS.

I'M A FUGITIVE, YOU KNOW. GOTTA BE CAREFUL.

I KNOW.

NOW THAT YOU'VE MADE IT THIS FAR, YOU MAY LIVE TO REGRET THIS STORY.

WELL, LET'S GET STARTED.

WHAT IS ANONYMOUS?

KLIK!

WHAT'S ANONYMOUS? OR WHO'S ANONYMOUS?

ANONYMOUS IS NOT A GROUP, AND IT'S NOT A PERSON.

SPECIFICALLY, IT IS THE IDEA THAT ALL OF US DESERVE FREEDOM.

FREEDOM OF THOUGHT, OF SPEECH, OF EXPRESSION, OF KNOWLEDGE, OF BELIEF.

THE FREEDOM TO DETERMINE THE COURSE AND DESTINATION OF OUR OWN LIVES.

IF YOU SHARE THIS IDEA, THEN YOU ARE ANONYMOUS.

YOU HAVE LIKELY HEARD MANY THINGS ABOUT ANONYMOUS.

SOME OF THEM ARE TRUE AND SOME OF THEM ARE NOT.

WE ARE NOT TERRORISTS, OR VIOLENT.

WE ARE CITIZENS OF THE WORLD WHO BEAR WITNESS TO TYRANNY, OPPRESSION, AND CENSORSHIP.

WE ARE ACTIVISTS WHO SEEK TO CHANGE THE SYSTEM AND THE CYCLE OF CORRUPTION.

WE SEEK TO CREATE TRANSPARENCY IN GOVERNMENTS AND ALL INSTITUTIONS OF PUBLIC SERVICE.

WE RESIST THOSE WHO SEEK TO VIOLATE OUR RIGHTS AS HUMAN BEINGS.

AS A COLLECTIVE OF AUTONOMOUS INDIVIDUALS, HOWEVER, WE HAVE NO LEADERS WHO DICTATE THE METHODS OF RESISTANCE.

SOME OF US ARE INDEED HACKERS, AND USE OUR SKILLS TO MAKE CRITICAL INFORMATION AVAILABLE TO THE PUBLIC.

SOME OF US ORGANIZE PROTESTS AND RALLIES.

SOME OF US VOLUNTEER OUR TIME TO FEED THOSE WHO CAN'T FEED THEMSELVES.

WE ARE YOUR NEIGHBORS, YOUR FRIENDS, AND YOUR RELATIVES.

WE PREPARE YOUR FOOD, REPAIR YOUR APPLIANCES, WRITE YOUR BOOKS, COMPOSE YOUR MUSIC, AND CREATE YOUR TECHNOLOGY.

WE ARE YOUR POSTAL WORKERS, BARBERS, STORE CLERKS, AND LAWYERS.

WE ARE SOCIALISTS AND CAPITALISTS. WE ARE ATHE- ISTS, AND WE ARE RELIGIOUS.

WE ARE EVERYONE, AND WE ARE NO ONE.

NONE OF US IS AS POWERFUL AS ALL OF US.

I GUESS THERE'S REALLY NO EASY WAY TO DEFINE IT.

NOT REALLY.

SO LET'S GO BACK TO THE BEGINNING.

15

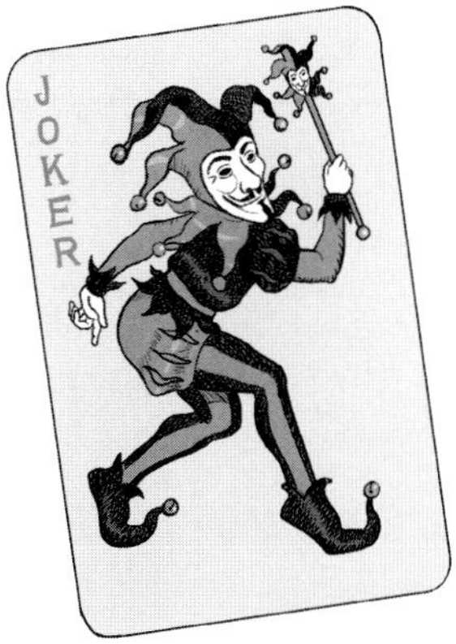
JOKER

CHAPTER 2

SO GOING BACK TO THE BEGINNING.

FROM WHAT I CAN GATHER, THE CULT OF THE DEAD COW WERE BASICALLY THE FIRST HACKTIVISTS, RIGHT?

HAHA, YEAH, "HACKTIVISM" WASN'T EVEN A THING WHEN THEY STARTED.

IN THE MID-1980S, LONG BEFORE ANONYMOUS HAD A NAME, THE TEENAGE FOUNDERS OF THE GROUP THAT WOULD BECOME KNOWN AS THE CULT OF THE DEAD COW HAD AN UNUSUAL HANGOUT SPOT.

... AN OLD SLAUGHTERHOUSE IN LUBBOCK, TEXAS.

THEY WERE CODERS, HOBBYISTS, AND ACTIVISTS EMPOWERED BY THE RISE OF PERSONAL COMPUTERS. THEY WANTED TO MESS AROUND AND HAVE FUN, BUT THEY WERE ALSO INTERESTED IN USING THEIR PCS FOR SOCIAL CHANGE.

WE NEED A NAME FOR OUR GROUP.

NAME?

CODE WARRIORS?

MACHINE HEADS?

SLAUGH-TERHOUSE FIVE?

NAME?

TAKEN.

THE CULT OF THE DEAD COW.

I LIKE THE SOUND OF IT!

CULT OF THE DEAD COW

C.D.C

ONE OF CDC'S HIGHEST-PROFILE TARGETS WAS THE CHURCH OF SCIENTOLOGY.

SCIENTOLOGY

THIS INTERNET FORUM IS MAKING A MOCKERY OF US!

WHAT SHOULD WE DO?

CALL THE INTERNET. HAVE IT ELIMINATED.

LUBBOCK, TEXAS, THE FOLLOWING WEEK.

DUDE, WHAT HAPPENED TO THE SCIENTOLOGY FORUM?

FUCKERS THINK THEY CONTROL THE INTERNET.

THIS IS CENSORSHIP. WE'VE GOTTA DO SOMETHING.

THE FORUM, IT'S BACK UP?

YES, LEADER.

I THOUGHT YOU TOLD THE INTERNET TO STOP!

WE DID!

WHO ARE "THE CULT OF THE DEAD COW"? SATANISTS?

"IN ORDER TO PRESERVE OUR WAY OF LIFE AND KEEP THE TORCH OF FREEDOM LIT FOR FUTURE GENERATIONS, WE FEEL IT IS OUR DUTY AS RESPONSIBLE WORLD CITIZENS TO DECLARE WAR ON THE SO-CALLED CHURCH OF SCIENTOLOGY."

HA! WE SHOWED THOSE IDIOTS! NO ONE LORDS OVER THE INTERNET.

WE NEED A NAME FOR THIS ... FOR WHAT WE'RE DOING!

OVER THE NEXT SEVERAL YEARS, HACKTIVISM QUICKLY SPREAD AROUND THE WORLD AS A NEW FORM OF POLITICAL PROTEST.

HACKTIVISM

IN CHINA, A GROUP OF DISSIDENTS WHO FREQUENTED CDC'S SITE THREATENED TO HACK U.S. COMPANIES WHO DID BUSINESS WITH THEIR COUNTRY. MUCH OF THE ACTION TOOK THE FORM OF ONLINE GRAFFITI.

HACKERS DEFACED THE INDIAN GOVERNMENT WEB-SITE WITH THE WORDS "SAVE KASHMIR" AND "MASSACRE," ALONG WITH PHOTOS OF KASHMIRIS ALLEGEDLY KILLED BY INDIA'S MILITARY.

TO PROTEST HUMAN RIGHTS VIOLATIONS, PORTUGUESE HACKERS DISPLAYED THE WORDS "FREE EAST TIMOR" ACROSS A SERIES OF SITES IN INDONESIA.

IN 1997, RICARDO DOMINGUEZ, AN ACTIVIST LIVING IN NYC, COFOUNDED A HACKTIVIST GROUP CALLED THE ELECTRONIC DISTURBANCE THEATER.

WAIT 'TIL YOU GUYS SEE THIS NEW CODE!

YOU CAUSING TROUBLE AGAIN?

DOMINGUEZ CREATED FLOODNET,

A COMPUTER PROGRAM DESIGNED TO SLOW DOWN OR EVEN CRASH WEBSITES WITH TRAFFIC.

HE USED THE TACTIC TO SWAMP MEXICAN GOVERNMENT WEBSITES TO SUPPORT ZAPATISTA REBELS.

DURING A RALLY IN THE EAST VILLAGE OF NEW YORK CITY IN 1998, STEFAN WRAY, A COLLEAGUE OF DOMINGUEZ, DECLARED A NEW MOVEMENT.

THIS IS A FORM OF ELECTRONIC CIVIL DISOBEDIENCE!

WE ARE TRANSFERRING THE SOCIAL MOVEMENT TACTICS OF TRESPASS AND BLOCKADE TO THE INTERNET.

AS HACKTIVISM BEGAN TO MAKE WAVES, FIGURES IN THE FBI AND CIA STARTED TO REGARD THE MOVEMENT WITH GROWING CONCERN.

WHAT DO YOU THINK ABOUT THESE ACTIVIST HACKERS?

WHAT THEY ARE DOING IS IMMORAL!

THEY WERE RIGHT TO WORRY.

SOMETHING BIG WAS RISING OUT OF A SHADOWY CORNER OF THE INTERNET.

4chan

LATE ONE FALL NIGHT IN 2003, CHRISTOPHER "MOOT" POOLE, A FIFTEEN-YEAR-OLD INSOMNIAC IN THE HUDSON VALLEY OF NEW YORK WAS SPENDING ANOTHER SLEEP-LESS NIGHT IN HIS ROOM.

MOOT DECIDED TO CRE-ATE A WEBSITE FOR FANS OF JAPANESE ANIMATION.

HE MODELED IT ON SITES IN JAPAN CALLED IMAGE BOARDS, WHICH LET PEOPLE POST AND COMMENT ON PICTURES WITHOUT HAVING TO REGISTER OR DISCLOSE THEIR NAMES.

HE CALLED HIS SITE 4CHAN.

VISITORS WHO DIDN'T SELECT A NICKNAME IN THE 4CHAN FORUMS WERE GIVEN THE DEFAULT HANDLE: ANONYMOUS.

ER.NAME

SSWORD

WE HAVE NO INTENTION OF PARTAKING IN INTEL-LIGENT DISCUSSIONS CONCERNING FOREIGN AFFAIRS.

I WANT 4CHAN TO BE FUN!

I CAN HAS CHEEZBURGER?

THE SITE QUICKLY SPIRALED BEYOND ANIME TO SPAWN MANY OF THE INTERNET'S EARLIEST INSIDE JOKES, OR MEMES.

NEVER GONNA GIVE YOU UP
NEVER GONNA LET YOU DOWN
NEVER GONNA RUN AROUND
AND DESERT YOU

THE MOST SHOCKING MEMES, OFTEN PORNOGRAPHIC OR SCATOLOGICAL, WERE POSTED IN A PORTION OF THE SITE DEVOTED TO RANDOM IMAGES AND LABELED "/B/."

THOUGH SOME REFERRED TO THEMSELVES AS /B/TARDS, THEY ALSO ADOPTED THEIR FORUM HANDLES AS THEIR COLLECTIVE MONIKER.

IN THAT MOMENT, ANONYMOUS WAS BORN.

LIKE A FACELESS, LEADERLESS GANG, ANONYMOUS STARTED OUT BY DOING PRANKS AND PROTESTS THEY CALLED "RAIDS."

ON JULY 12, 2006, ANONYMOUS VENTURED OFF 4CHAN FOR ONE OF THEIR FIRST RAIDS.

IT WAS AGAINST A FINNISH VIRTUAL WORLD FOR CHILDREN CALLED "HABBO HOTEL."

HABBO

OSTENSIBLY, THE RAID WAS DONE IN RESPONSE TO A RUMOR THAT THE SITE'S CREATORS HAD BANNED THE USE OF DARK-SKINNED AVATARS.

POOL CLOSED DUE TO AIDS!

BUT IT WAS ALSO FOR THE "LULZ," INTERNET SLANG FOR THE ACRONYM LOL, OR "LAUGH OUT LOUD."

LOLZ!

THE PRANKS COMPETED FOR SHOCK VALUE AND BEGAN GARNERING NATIONAL ATTENTION.

ONE ANON THREATENED TO BLOW UP FOOT-BALL STADIUMS, AND WAS ARRESTED BY THE FBI.

FBI

FBI

ANOTHER POSTED A MESSAGE ON 4CHAN DETAILING HIS PLANS FOR A HIGH SCHOOL SHOOTING.

IN THE SUMMER OF 2007, FOX TV NEWS RAN ONE OF THE FIRST REPORTS ON THE GROUP, SETTING THE TONE FOR THE SENSATIONAL COVERAGE TO COME.

ANONYMOUS

FOX
11
NEWS

THEY CALL THEMSELVES ANONYMOUS. THEY ARE HACKERS ON STEROIDS, TREATING THE WEB LIKE A REAL-LIFE VIDEO GAME.

THEY ATTACK INNOCENT PEOPLE, LIKE AN INTERNET HATE MACHINE.

ANONYMOUS

THIS MOTHER'S FIGHTING ANONYMOUS. HER WHOLE FAMILY'S BEEN UNDER ATTACK . . .

SHE INSTALLED ELECTRONIC SECURITY, A PHONE TRACING SYSTEM, AND BOUGHT A DOG.

BUT ANONYMOUS DIDN'T STOP THERE.

THEY FLOODED A WHITE SUPREMACIST'S PODCAST WITH PHONY PHONE CALLS AND TOOK DOWN HIS SITE.

THERE'S NO MIKE HUNT HERE!

THEY BEGAN OUTING AND ATTACKING PEDOPHILES ONLINE.

BUT EARLY IN 2008, ANONYMOUS FOUND THEIR BIGGEST TARGET YET: THE SAME ONE THAT THE CULT OF THE DEAD COW HAD GONE AFTER A DECADE BEFORE.

THE CHURCH OF SCIENTOLOGY.

SCIENTOLOGY

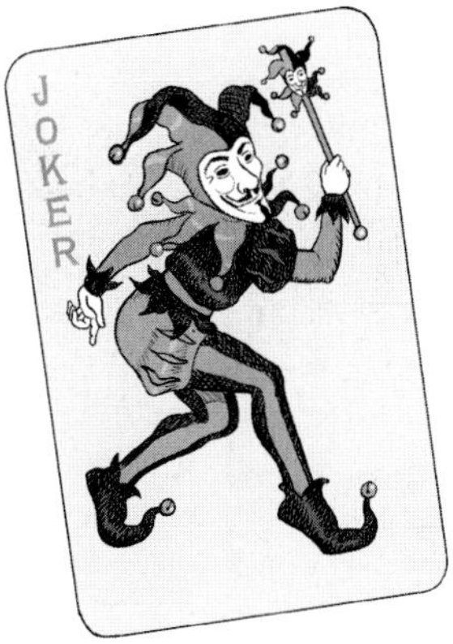
JOKER

CHAPTER 3

I SHOULD QUIT ONE OF THESE DAYS.

SO LET ME GET THIS STRAIGHT: YOU GREW UP IN MAINE ON A HORSE RANCH.

RAN AWAY FROM HOME IN YOUR TEENS.

CORRECT.

I ENDED UP IN CAMBRIDGE SLEEPING ON BENCHES AND HANGING OUT WITH HACKERS AND ACTIVISTS IN THE 1980S.

WHEN DID ANONYMOUS START HAVING A LARGER PRESENCE IN THE HACKTIVIST COMMUNITY?

SCIENTOLOGY! I HEARD ABOUT IT ONLINE. AND IT BLEW MY FUCKING MIND!

AT 2 A.M. ON JANUARY 14, 2008, A 9-MINUTE, 26-SECOND CLIP APPEARED ON YOUTUBE WITH THE SEEMINGLY BENIGN TITLE "TOM CRUISE SCIENTOLOGY VIDEO."

IN THE VIDEO, INTENDED AS AN INTERNAL PIECE OF CHURCH PROPAGANDA, THE STAR OF "RISKY BUSINESS" AND "TOP GUN" TURNS EARNEST AND FANATICAL.

BEING A SCIENTOLOGIST, WHEN YOU DRIVE PAST AN ACCIDENT, IT'S NOT LIKE ANYONE ELSE.

AS YOU DRIVE PAST, YOU KNOW YOU HAVE TO DO SOMETHING ABOUT IT BECAUSE YOU KNOW YOU'RE THE ONLY ONE THAT CAN REALLY HELP.

WE ARE THE AUTHORITIES ON THE MIND.

DAYS EARLIER MARC EBNER, A JOURNALIST WHO HAD WRITTEN ABOUT SCIENTOLOGY FOR MANY YEARS, HAD LEAKED THE VIDEO AND URGENTLY EMAILED ALL HIS FRIENDS ABOUT IT.

HOLY CRAP! THIS IS INCREDIBLE!

NICK DENTON, THE EDITOR OF THE GOSSIP SITE GAWKER, LOVED THE CLIPS AND GUSHINGLY POSTED A LINK TO THE VIDEO.

IF TOM CRUISE JUMPING ON OPRAH'S COUCH WAS AN EIGHT ON THE SCALE OF SCARY, THIS IS A TEN!

ALMOST IMMEDIATELY, THE VIDEO WAS EVERYWHERE.

THEN IT VANISHED, REPLACED BY AN OFFICIAL MESSAGE FROM THE CHURCH OF SCIENTOLOGY.

This video is no longer available due to a copyright claim by the Church of Scientology.

MEANWHILE ON 4CHAN ANONYMOUS FELT EMBOLDENED BY ITS RECENT ACCOMPLISHMENTS.

I THINK IT'S TIME FOR /B/ TO DO SOMETHING BIG.

I'M TALKING ABOUT HACKING OR TAKING DOWN THE OFFICIAL SCIENTOLOGY WEBSITE.

IT'S TIME TO USE OUR RESOURCES TO DO SOMETHING WE BELIEVE IS RIGHT.

TALK AMONGST ONE ANOTHER, FIND A BETTER PLACE TO PLAN IT, AND THEN CARRY OUT WHAT CAN AND MUST BE DONE.

FOR SEVERAL DAYS, ANONYMOUS DEBATED HOW THEY MIGHT STRIKE.

MISSION IMPOSSIBLE. A RANDOM IMAGE BOARD CAN'T TAKE DOWN A PSEUDO-RELIGION WITH THE BACKING OF WEALTHY PEOPLE AND AN ARMY OF LAWYERS.

DON'T GET INVOLVED IF YOU DON'T THINK IT'S POSSIBLE!

START SMALL, ANON. THE WEBSITE, FIRST. MAYBE RAID THE FORUMS, ETC.

WE ARE THOUSANDS STRONG, THEY CAN'T SUE ALL OF US.

SOUNDS GOOD. LET THE RAID COMMENCE.

INITIALLY, THE RESPONSE TOOK THE FORM OF TYPICAL RAIDS.

ERROR-404

SCIENTOLOGY WEBSITES WERE HACKED AND OVERWHELMED WITH PHANTOM USERS.

ENDLESS "BLACK FAXES," PAGES FILLED ENTIRELY WITH A UNIFORM BLACK TONE, SPOOLED THROUGH SCIENTOLOGY FAX MACHINES, DEPLETING INK CARTRIDGES AND RENDERING THE MACHINES USELESS.

PIZZAS ARRIVED AT CHURCHES AROUND THE WORLD, INCLUDING A REPORTED THREE HUNDRED AT THE HEADQUARTERS IN AMSTERDAM ALONE.

ANONYMOUS SPAMMED THE INTERNET WITH THE MOST OUTLANDISH STORIES THEY COULD FIND ABOUT SCIENTOLOGY.

NEW YORK POST

SCIENTOLOGY SEX ASSAULT NIGHTMARE

FORMER Scientology staffer is breaking her silen about being sexually assaulted 100 times at age church supervisor she was "order iving threats and i abuse.

FINALLY, ON JANUARY 21, AFTER SEVERAL DAYS HONING THE VIDEO, THE "MESSAGE TO SCIENTOLOGY" HIT YOUTUBE LIKE SOME MASH-UP OF NINE INCH NAILS AND 1984.

IN A CRYPTIC, COMPUTERIZED VOICE-OVER, ANONYMOUS LET THEIR MISSION BE KNOWN.

We acknowledge you as a serious opponent, and we are prepared for a long, long campaign.

You will not prevail forever against the angry masses of the body politic.

Your methods, hypocrisy, and the artlessness of your organization have sounded its death knell.

You cannot hide. We are everywhere.

WITHIN FOUR DAYS, "MESSAGE TO SCIENTOLOGY" HAD RACKED UP 800,000 VIEWS.

0:57 / 2:03

Message to Scientology

5,365,636 views

ChurchOfScientology
Published on Jan 21, 2008

IN THE MEANTIME SOME OF THE MORE NEFARIOUS ELEMENTS OF ANONYMOUS SEEMED TO BE ACTING OUT ON THEIR OWN.

POOF!

TWENTY-FOUR SCIENTOLOGY CENTERS IN CALIFORNIA HAVE RECEIVED SUSPICIOUS PACKAGES OF WHITE POWDER.

FBI OFFICES, LOS ANGELES

WE DEMAND THE FBI INVESTIGATE ANONYMOUS!

WE'LL SEE WHAT WE CAN DO.

THE SCIENTOLOGY PR MACHINE BEGAN PUSHING THEIR AGENDA TO THE PRESS.

THEY ARE CYBER-TERRORISTS WHO HIDE THEIR IDENTITIES BEHIND MASKS AND COMPUTER ANONYMITY.

ON JANUARY 27, MARK BUNKER, A WRY AND AVUNCULAR TV PRODUCER WHO HAD BEEN FIGHTING THE CHURCH FOR A DECADE, POSTED A MESSAGE TO ANONYMOUS ON YOUTUBE.

THE TACTICS ANONYMOUS IS USING, LIKE SHUTTING DOWN SCIENTOLOGY WEBSITES, ARE HORRIBLY WRONG.

HE CHALLENGED THE GROUP TO PUT ASIDE THE HACKER TRICKS AND FOCUS ON POLITICAL ACTION.

ANONYMOUS EMBRACED BUNKER AND HIS MESSAGE, AND GAVE HIM AN AFFECTIONATE NICKNAME.

MARK BUNKER, WE HEREBY DUB THEE "WISE BEARD MAN."

THE DAY OF BUNKER'S MESSAGE, A NEW VIDEO APPEARED ON YOUTUBE UNDER THE HEADING "A CALL TO ACTION."

Be very wary of the 10th of February.

You have nowhere to hide because we are everywhere.

We are Anonymous.

THE PLAN: TO TAKE THEIR FOLLOWERS TO THE STREETS IN A SERIES OF PROTESTS AT SCIENTOLOGY HEADQUARTERS.

BUT FEARING THE CHURCH'S REPUTATION FOR TARGETING CRITICS, THE GROUP NEEDED A WAY TO REMAIN ANONYMOUS IN PUBLIC.

HOW DO WE OPERATE IN PLAIN SIGHT WITHOUT RISKING THE PIGS GETTING THE AUTHORITIES ON OUR CASE?

WE CAN WEAR MASKS!

HOW ABOUT BATMAN MASKS?

OR ALFRED E. NEUMAN!

HOW ABOUT THE MASK FROM THAT MOVIE "V FOR VENDETTA"?

IT WAS A COMIC BOOK FIRST, IDIOT.

GUY FAWKES! GOOD IDEA, IT'S AVAILABLE EVERY-WHERE, IN LARGE QUANTITIES, AND FOR CHEAP.

IN HUNDREDS OF CITIES ACROSS THE GLOBE, THOUSANDS OF PROTESTERS GATHERED DRESSED IN OUTLANDISH COSTUMES.

OUTSIDE THE SCIENTOLOGY CHURCH IN HOLLYWOOD, BUNKER, EBNER, AND OTHER OLD-SCHOOL OPPONENTS OF THE RELIGION JOINED ANONYMOUS.

SCIENTOLOGY DESTROYS FAMILIES!

SCIENTOLOGY BULLIES! LUNATICS! SCAMMERS!

THE CULT OF $CIENTOLOGY IS A $CAM

IT WAS ONLY A MATTER OF TIME BEFORE SCIENTOLOGY STRUCK BACK.

THESE DAMN S.P.S!

TO INFORM ANONYMOUS MEMBERS WHO MAY BE UNAWARE OF THE CRIMINAL ACTS COMMITTED BY THEIR LEADERS, AND TO PREVENT OTHERS FROM BEING MIS-LED BY ANONYMOUS PROPAGANDA, WE HAVE PRODUCED A VIDEO TO PROVIDE THE FACTS.

WHILE CLAIMING THEY ARE PEACEFUL, IN LESS THAN THREE WEEKS ANONYMOUS MEMBERS MADE OR ENCOURAGED 8,139 HARASSING OR THREATENING PHONE CALLS AND 3.6 MILLION MALICIOUS EMAILS.

CLAIMS OF ALTRUISTIC PURPOSES ENUNCIATED IN ANONYMOUS'S STATEMENTS TO THE PRESS ARE NO DIF-FERENT THAN THOSE MADE BY ANY CYBERTERRORIST OR HATE GROUP.

ON MARCH 15, 2008, CHOSEN TO COINCIDE WITH L. RON HUBBARD BIRTHDAY CELEBRATIONS, SEVERAL THOUSAND ANONS MARCHED PAST SCIENTOLOGY CHURCHES IN MORE THAN A HUNDRED CITIES, FROM LONDON TO SYDNEY.

ONE OF THE BIGGEST PROTESTS TOOK PLACE OUTSIDE THE CHURCH OF SCIENTOLOGY IN HOLLYWOOD.

SCIENTOLOGY

TAX THE CULT! TAX THE CULT!

HONK IF SCIENTOLOGY IS A CULT!

HONK! HONK!

WHY ARE YOU HERE?

ANONYMOUS IS OUR GENERATION'S MOVEMENT. EVERY FORTY YEARS SOMEONE STANDS UP AND DOES SOMETHING!

THIS IS OUR GENERATION'S WAY OF DOING SOMETHING!

BUT BEFORE LONG, PANIC SET IN.

A GUN!

THERE'S A GUY WITH A GUN!

WHY WOULD YOU BRING A GUN TO A PEACEFUL PROTEST?

I'M NOT HERE FOR A PEACEFUL PROTEST, FRIEND.

WELL, YOU GOT PEOPLE UPSET BECAUSE YOU'RE BRANDISHING A GUN.

I'M NOT BRANDISHING ANYTHING.

SCIENTOLOGY IS A SCAM!

43

IN THE DAYS AND WEEKS AFTER THE PROTESTS, ANONYMOUS DID NOT "DISMANTLE" THE CHURCH OF SCIENTOLOGY.

SCIENTOLOGY

BUT THE TOM CRUISE VIDEO REMAINED ONLINE.

FOR ANONYMOUS, IT FELT LIKE A WIN.

THEY BEGAN PLOTTING HOW TO PROTEST OTHER TARGETS-- POLITICIANS, WARMONGERS, POLLUTERS--AND ADOPTED A BOMBASTIC SLOGAN.

We are Legion.

We do not forgive.

We do not forget.

Expect us.

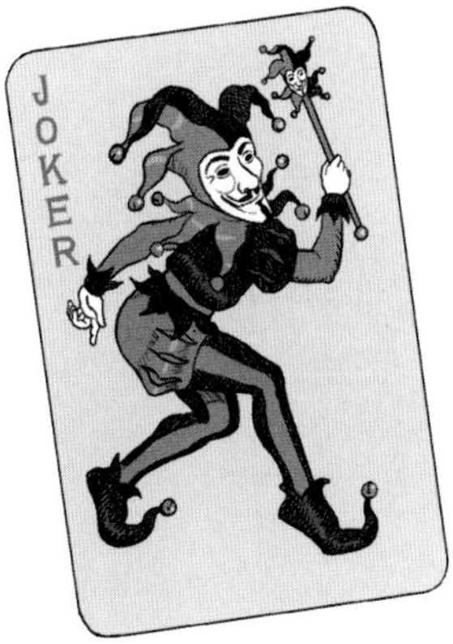
JOKER

CHAPTER 4

HOW'S BUSINESS, BROTHER?

ALMOST GOT ENOUGH FOR THAT YACHT.

STAY STRONG!

SO LET'S PICK UP THE STORY AGAIN.

SHOOT.

AFTER SCIENTOLOGY, THERE WAS THE BIG DUSTUP WITH SONY.

WHAT A SHIT SHOW.

IT ALL STARTED WITH GEOHOT.

ON JANUARY 23, 2010, GEORGE "GEOHOT" HOTZ, A TWENTY-YEAR-OLD FROM NEW JERSEY, WAS TYPING FURIOUSLY ON HIS BLOG.

HE HAD A SHOCKING ANNOUNCEMENT:

I have hacked the PS3!

HE LATER POSTED INSTRUCTIONS FOR OTHERS TO DO THE SAME, AND FREELY DISTRIBUTED THE CODE TO HELP THEM.

NOTHING IS UNHACKABLE!

I CAN NOW DO WHATEVER I WANT WITH THE SYSTEM.

IT'S LIKE I'VE GOT AN AWESOME NEW POWER. I'M JUST NOT SURE HOW TO WIELD IT.

HOTZ HAD ENABLED THE PS3 TO RUN LINUX, AN ALTERNATIVE OPERATING SYSTEM. THIS ESSENTIALLY TURNED THE PS3 FROM A SINGLE-PURPOSE GAMING CONSOLE INTO A DESKTOP COMPUTER, WHICH PEOPLE COULD USE TO WRITE PROGRAMS.

LITTLE DID HE KNOW HE WAS ABOUT TO TRIGGER ONE OF ANONYMOUS'S MOST NOTORIOUS WARS.

FREE GEOHOT!

I AM GEOHOT

SONY RESPONDED BY RELEASING A SOFTWARE UPDATE THAT DISABLED HOTZ'S EFFORTS.

COME ON PEOPLE, WE NEED TO GET THIS PATCH READY BY MIDNIGHT!

GAMERS AND HACKERS WERE FURIOUS THAT SONY HAD ROBBED THEM OF THEIR ABILITY TO USE THE PS3 LIKE A COMPUTER.

I am EXTREMELY upset.

SOME WANTED TO RALLY AROUND HOTZ AND ORGANIZE.

THIS IS MADNESS!!! HACKERS UNITE!!! GEOHOT WILL LEAD US INTO THE LIGHT!

BUT MANY WERE ANGRY AT HOTZ, NOT AT SONY.

Congratulations, Geohot, the asshole who sits at home doing nothing other than ruining the experience for others.

SOMEONE POSTED HOTZ'S PHONE NUMBER ONLINE, AND HARASSING CALLS ENSUED.

WE KNOW WHERE YOU LIVE, DIPSHIT!

IN LATE DECEMBER, HOTZ DECIDED ONCE AGAIN TO HACK THE PS3.

HE HAD TRIED ONCE BEFORE, ONLY TO BE THWARTED BY SONY, BUT NOT THIS TIME.

HIS NEW CODE WORKED, AND IT WAS READY TO BE RELEASED TO THE WORLD.

SONY HAD ALSO LONG BOASTED ABOUT THE SECURITY OF THE PS3.

HOTZ WAS ABOUT TO PROVE THEM WRONG.

HE WAS ABOUT TO UNDO YEARS OF CORPORATE PR AND POTENTIALLY OPEN THE DOOR TO PIRACY.

REALIZING THIS, HE WROTE CODE THAT DISABLED THE ABILITY TO RUN PIRATED SOFTWARE USING HIS HACK.

STILL, HE WANTED A SECOND OPINION.

BEFORE HE PUT THE CODE LIVE, HE SIGNED INTO AN ONLINE CHAT CHANNEL WHERE HACKER FRIENDS HUNG OUT AND ASKED THEM WHETHER HE SHOULD RELEASE HIS HACK.

Yeah. Information should be free.

WELL, THERE YOU GO!

HOTZ RELEASED THE CODE, THEN WENT TO SLEEP.

49

THE FOLLOWING DAY HOTZ WOKE UP TO A MESSAGE FROM SONY'S LAWYERS.

OH CRAP!

ON JANUARY 14, HOTZ WENT ON "ATTACK OF THE SHOW," A POPULAR NEWS PROGRAM FOR GAMERS.

THE LOOP

WE ARE HERE TODAY WITH INFAMOUS HACKER GEOHOT, WHO IS BEING SUED BY SONY!

SO WHAT ARE YOU BEING SUED FOR?

MAKING SONY MAD.

I THINK THIS CASE IS ABOUT A LOT MORE THAN WHAT I DID, OR ME.

IT'S ABOUT WHETHER YOU REALLY OWN THAT DEVICE THAT YOU PURCHASED.

LATER, HE UPLOADED A HIP-HOP VIDEO ON YOUTUBE THAT HE TITLED "THE LIGHT IT UP CONTEST."

CLIK!

YO, IT'S GEOHOT, AND FOR THOSE THAT DON'T KNOW, I'M GETTING SUED BY SONY.

THOUGHT YOU'D TACKLE THIS WITH A LITTLE MORE TACT, BUT THEN AGAIN, FUDGEPACKERS, I DON'T KNOW JACK.

BUT SHIT MAN, THEY'RE A CORPORA-TION, AND I'M A PERSONIFICATION . . . OF FREEDOM FOR ALL.

EXHIBIT THIS IN THE COURTROOM. GO ON, DO IT, I DARE YOU.

HOTZ'S CATCHY RAP EARNED HIM SYMPATHY IN CHAT ROOMS BUT NOT IN THE COURTS.

A CALIFORNIA DISTRICT COURT GRANTED SONY THE RESTRAINING ORDER AGAINST HOTZ, PREVENTING HIM FROM HACKING AND DISSEMINATING MORE DETAILS ABOUT ITS MACHINES.

IT ALSO APPROVED A REQUEST BY SONY TO SUBPOENA INFORMATION FROM TWITTER, GOOGLE, YOUTUBE, AND BLUEHOST, HOTZ'S INTERNET PROVIDER, INCLUDING THE INTERNET PROTOCOL ADDRESSES OF ANYONE WHO DOWNLOADED THE INSTRUCTIONS FROM HIS SITE, A MOVE THAT FURTHER INCENSED DIGITAL-RIGHTS ADVOCATES.

SONY ALSO GAINED ACCESS TO RECORDS FROM HOTZ'S PAYPAL ACCOUNT.

IN SOME CIRCLES, THE REBEL LEADER WAS BECOMING A MARTYR.

LEAVE GEOHOT ALONE!

GEOHOT = SAVIOR OF MANKIND

MARTYRS WIN DEVOTEES, AND SOON HOTZ HAD GAINED THE ALLEGIANCE OF THE MOST NOTORIOUS HACKERS:

STAND WITH GEOHOT!

ANONYMOUS.

WELCOME! #opsony

IN EARLY APRIL, AN ANONYMOUS MEMBER CREATED AN INTERNET RELAY CHAT ROOM CALLED OPERATION SONY, OR #OPSONY.

IT IS THE DUTY OF ANONYMOUS TO HELP OUT THIS YOUNG LAD, AND TO PROTEST AGAINST SONY'S CENSORSHIP.

I DUG UP SOME GOOD INFO ON SONY.

9166

01

LET'S HAVE FLASH MOBS OUTSIDE SONY STORES!

4181

OR SEND BLACK FAXES TO WASTE ALL THE INK IN THEIR MACHINES!

2164

Congratulations, Sony. You have now received the undivided attention of Anonymous.

You must face the consequences of your actions, Anonymous style.

You saw a hornet's nest, and stuck your penises in it.

WITHIN HOURS, BOTH SONY.COM AND PLAYSTATION.COM WERE DOWN. ANONYMOUS POSTED A VIDEO ON YOUTUBE WITH ITS DEMANDS.

Drop the case against Hotz and allow for modifications on the PS3.

INTERNET PROTESTS, LIKE STREET PROTESTS, CAN SPIN OUT OF CONTROL.

NO SOONER HAD THE HACKER WAR BEGUN THAN ONE ANON DECLARED A SPLINTER FACTION.

I'M STARTING SONYRECON!

IT'S TIME FOR PERSONAL ATTACKS AGAINST SONY EMPLOYEES AND THE JUDGE IN THE GEOHOT CASE.

LET'S POST ALL THE SONY EXECS' PERSONAL INFO!

I'VE GOT THE CEO'S HOME ADDRESS!

WE'LL SHIT ON HIS DOORSTEP, THEN RUN AWAY.

LOL! LOL!

BACK IN HIS PARENTS' HOUSE, HOTZ CLICKS WITH MOUNTING APPREHENSION THROUGH THE NEWS OF ANONYMOUS'S PLANS.

OH MAN!

I HOPE TO GOD SONY DOESN'T THINK THIS IS ME.

I'M THE COMPLETE OPPOSITE OF ANONYMOUS.

ON APRIL 11, SONY ANNOUNCED THAT IT HAD REACHED AN AGREEMENT WITH HOTZ, WHO DENIED WRONGDOING BUT CONSENTED TO A PERMANENT INJUNCTION BARRING HIM FROM REVERSE-ENGINEERING ANY SONY PRODUCT IN THE FUTURE.

BUT HOTZ'S SUPPORTERS FELT THAT THE INJUNCTION WAS A FORM OF CENSORSHIP.

OTHERS WENT TO SONY STORES IN CITIES SUCH AS SAN DIEGO AND COSTA MESA TO PROTEST.

At 4:15 P.M. on April 19, 2011, technicians at the San Diego offices of Sony Network Entertainment noticed that four of their computer servers were rebooting without authorization.

WHAT'S HAPPENING TO OUR SERVERS?

SOMEONE'S ACCESSED THE DATABASE!

QUICK! TAKE THE SYSTEMS OFFLINE!

NOTHING ON THIS LOG. 5999 MORE TO GO . . .

HOW BAD IS IT?

SIR, WE WERE THE VICTIM OF A SOPHISTICATED ATTACK.

THEY EXPOSED THE ADDRESSES, PASSWORDS, BIRTHDAYS, AND EMAIL ADDRESSES OF SEVENTY-SEVEN MILLION OF OUR SUBSCRIBERS.

57

PATRICK SEYBOLD, A COMPANY SPOKESMAN, TRIED TO REASSURE PLAYERS.

WHILE THERE IS NO EVIDENCE AT THIS TIME THAT CREDIT CARD DATA WAS TAKEN, WE CANNOT RULE OUT THE POSSIBILITY.

IT WAS NEVER CONFIRMED WHETHER ANONYMOUS WAS RESPONSIBLE FOR THE HACK OR IF SOMEONE ELSE SAW AN OPENING IN ALL THE CHAOS.

AT 4:51 A.M. ON APRIL 28, HOTZ UPLOADED A LENGTHY RANT AGAINST THE PSN HACKERS.

Running homebrew and exploring security on your devices is cool.

Hacking into someone else's server and stealing databases of user info is not cool.

You make the hacking community look bad, even if it is aimed at douches like Sony.

THE DATA BREACH ON THE SONY ONLINE ENTERTAINMENT SERVICE EXPOSED 24 MILLION PERSONAL ACCOUNTS.

TECHNICIANS ALSO FOUND A FILE THAT HAD BEEN PLANTED ON ONE OF THEIR SERVERS AS A KIND OF DIGITAL GRAFFITI.

we are legion

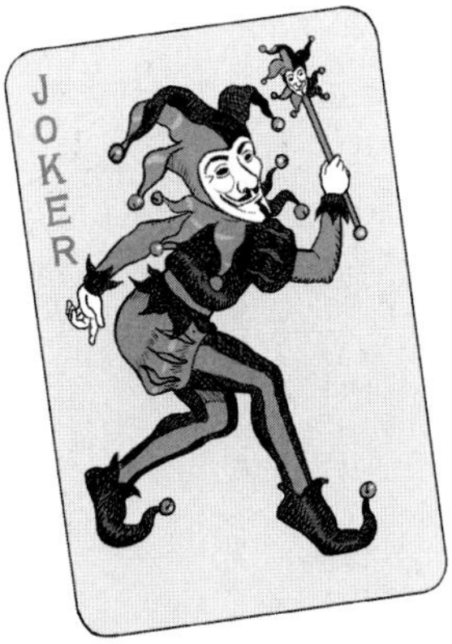
JOKER

CHAPTER 5

CAN I HELP YOU?

THE BIGGEST AND BLACKEST THING YOU GOT.

GOTTA BREAK THE PIGGY BANK FOR THIS ONE.

SO AROUND THE TIME OF THE SONY WAR, YOU WERE OUT IN SANTA CRUZ, RIGHT?

YEAH, YOU KNOW, LEFT BOSTON FOR THE WEST. BETTER WEATHER. AND WAY BETTER WEED.

IT WAS NICE AT FIRST. BUT THEN SHIT WENT BAD REAL FAST.

AROUND THE TIME THAT ANONYMOUS BATTLED SONY, COMMANDER X MOVED TO SANTA CRUZ, CALIFORNIA, TO JOIN A LOCAL MOVEMENT CALLED PEACE CAMP.

GOOD SPOT FOR A HOMEBASE.

NOT A VERY IMAGINATIVE PASSWORD, NEIGHBOR.

TO COMMANDER X, THIS WAS ACTIVISM MADE TANGIBLE.

PROTESTING AGAINST APARTHEID IN CAMBRIDGE, HE COULD NOT SEE IMMEDIATE RESULTS; NOW, WITH THE TAP OF A BUTTON, HE COULD HELP SABOTAGE A MAJOR CORPORATION'S SITE.

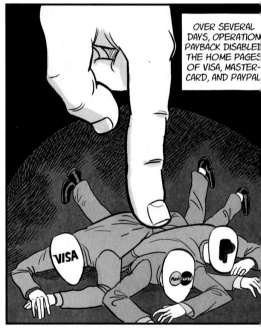

OVER SEVERAL DAYS, OPERATION PAYBACK DISABLED THE HOME PAGES OF VISA, MASTERCARD, AND PAYPAL

I COULD WIELD ANONYMOUS AGAINST THIS TINY LITTLE CITY GOVERNMENT AND THEY WOULD JUST BE FUCKING WRECKED.

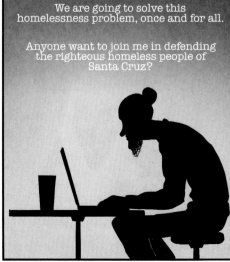

We are going to solve this homelessness problem, once and for all.

Anyone want to join me in defending the righteous homeless people of Santa Cruz?

MEANWHILE IN OHIO...

A TWENTY-FIVE-YEAR-OLD ANON WHO WORKED AS A RECEPTIONIST AT A COLLEGE AND WENT BY THE NICKNAME ABSOLEM ADMIRED COMMANDER X'S PASSION.

THOUGH HE KNEW NOTHING ABOUT SANTA CRUZ POLITICS, HE MESSAGED BACK TO ANONYMOUS IMMEDIATELY.

I'VE BEEN WAITING TO JOIN SOMETHING LIKE THIS MY ENTIRE LIFE.

WELCOME ABOARD, ABSOLEM!

ON DECEMBER 10, COMMANDER X EMAILED JOURNALISTS ABOUT HIS PLAN OF ACTION.

ATTENTION, MEDIA! AT EXACTLY NOON LOCAL TIME TOMORROW, THE PEOPLE'S LIBERATION FRONT AND ANONYMOUS WILL REMOVE FROM THE INTERNET THE WEBSITE OF THE SANTA CRUZ COUNTY GOVERNMENT.

AND EXACTLY THIRTY MINUTES LATER, WE WILL RETURN IT TO NORMAL FUNCTION.

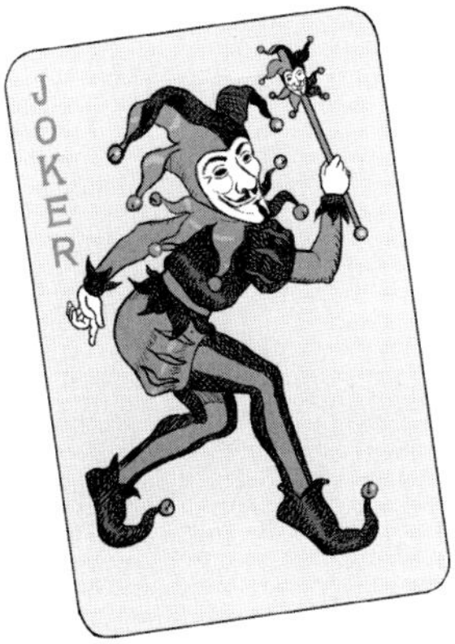
JOKER

CHAPTER 6

SNIFF!

THESE GUYS DON'T SCREW AROUND.

STUFF'S LIKE ROCKET FUEL.

NO KIDDING! I DON'T THINK I'LL BE SLEEPING TONIGHT.

OK, SO LET'S GET BACK TO THE STORY.

WAS IT HARD TO LEAVE SANTA CRUZ?

YEAH, BUT I KNEW I HAD TO HIT THE ROAD.

SAN FRAN OR BUST!

DARK ROAST, EXTRA LARGE.

ON THE RUN FROM THE FBI, COMMANDER X SETS UP SHOP IN HAIGHT-ASHBURY.

HEY GUYS, DID YOU MISS ME?

WELCOME BACK, X.

WHAT ARE WE GOING TO DO NEXT?

TUNISIA.

YEAH, IT'S A COUNTRY IN THE MIDDLE EAST. WHAT ABOUT IT?

WE'RE GONNA TAKE DOWN ITS DICTATOR.

OH, THEY HAVE A DICTATOR?

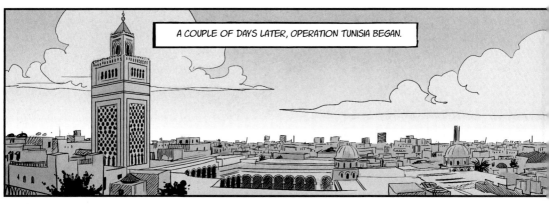

A COUPLE OF DAYS LATER, OPERATION TUNISIA BEGAN.

ANONYMOUS SPAMMED TUNISIAN GOVERNMENT EMAIL ADDRESSES IN AN ATTEMPT TO CLOG THEIR SERVERS.

IN ONE DAY, THE ANONS BROUGHT DOWN THE WEBSITES OF THE TUNISIAN STOCK EXCHANGE, THE MINISTRY OF INDUSTRY, THE PRESIDENT, AND THE PRIME MINISTER.

PAYBACK IS A BITCH.

ANONYMOUS-AFFILIATED OPERATIONS
CONTINUED TO BE ANNOUNCED ON YOUTUBE:

OPERATION LIBYA.

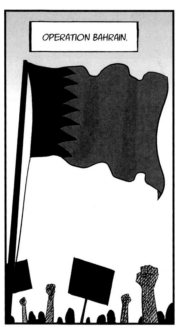

OPERATION BAHRAIN.

OPERATION MOROCCO.

AS PROTESTERS FILLED TAHRIR
SQUARE, ANONYMOUS PARTICIPATED
IN OPERATION EGYPT.

ON SEPTEMBER 22, 2011, IN A COFFEE SHOP IN MOUNTAIN VIEW, CALIFORNIA, COMMANDER X WAS ARRESTED AND CHARGED WITH CAUSING INTENTIONAL DAMAGE TO A PROTECTED COMPUTER.

HE WAS DETAINED FOR A WEEK AND RELEASED ON BOND.

AGAINST HIS LAWYER'S ADVICE, HE RETURNED TO SANTA CRUZ AND HELD A PRESS CONFERENCE ON THE STEPS OF THE COUNTY COURTHOUSE.

I AM IMMENSELY PROUD, AND HUMBLED TO THE CORE, TO BE A PART OF THE IDEA CALLED ANONYMOUS.

ALL YOU NEED TO BE A WORLD-CLASS HACKER IS A COMPUTER AND A COOL PAIR OF SUNGLASSES.

THE COMPUTER IS OPTIONAL.

THREE MONTHS LATER, COMMANDER X'S PRO-BONO LAWYER, JAY LEIDERMAN, WAS IN A FEDERAL COURT IN SAN JOSE.

IS THERE A REASON WHY YOUR CLIENT DID NOT SHOW UP FOR THIS TRIAL?

I'M AFRAID I'VE LOST TOUCH WITH MR X.

IT APPEARS AS THOUGH THE DEFENDANT HAS FLED.

BY EARLY 2012, THE UNITED STATES GOVERNMENT HAD ANONYMOUS IN ITS CROSSHAIRS.

KEITH ALEXANDER, THE NSA AND U.S. CYBER COMMAND DIRECTOR, HAD HELD CLASSIFIED MEETINGS TO EXPRESS CONCERN ABOUT ANONYMOUS.

WITHIN TWO YEARS, ANONYMOUS COULD BE CAPABLE OF DESTABILIZING POWER GRIDS!

THEY ARE BECOMING A REAL THREAT THAT NEEDS TO BE ADDRESSED.

GENERAL MARTIN DEMPSEY, THE CHAIRMAN OF THE JOINT CHIEFS OF STAFF, WARNED THAT AN ENEMY OF THE U.S. COULD WREAK HAVOC BY EXPLOITING ANONYMOUS.

A NEAR-PEER COMPETITOR COUNTRY COULD GIVE CYBER MALWARE CAPABILITY TO SOME FRINGE GROUP.

I DON'T THINK PEOPLE GET THAT ANYONE CAN BE ANONYMOUS.

ALL YOU GOTTA DO IS SAY YOU'RE IN, AND YOU'RE IN.

BY 2013, ANONYMOUS HAD BECOME A PURPOSEFULLY CHAOTIC AND LEADERLESS COLLECTIVE.

ANYONE COULD PROCLAIM THEMSELVES A MEMBER OR DECLARE AN OPERATION AGAINST A TARGET.

I'M ANONYMOUS.

I'M ANONYMOUS.

I'M ANONYMOUS.

BUT GETTING OTHERS TO CARE WAS ANOTHER STORY.

FOR EVERY ANON WHO SPAWNED A SUCCESSFUL OP AGAINST THE CHURCH OF SCIENTOLOGY OR THE SANTA CRUZ GOVERNMENT, COUNTLESS OTHERS WATCHED THEIR YOUTUBE MANIFESTOS DISAPPEAR IN A STREAM OF GRUMPY CATS.

THIS IS WHAT MADE KYANONYMOUS STAND OUT.

KY

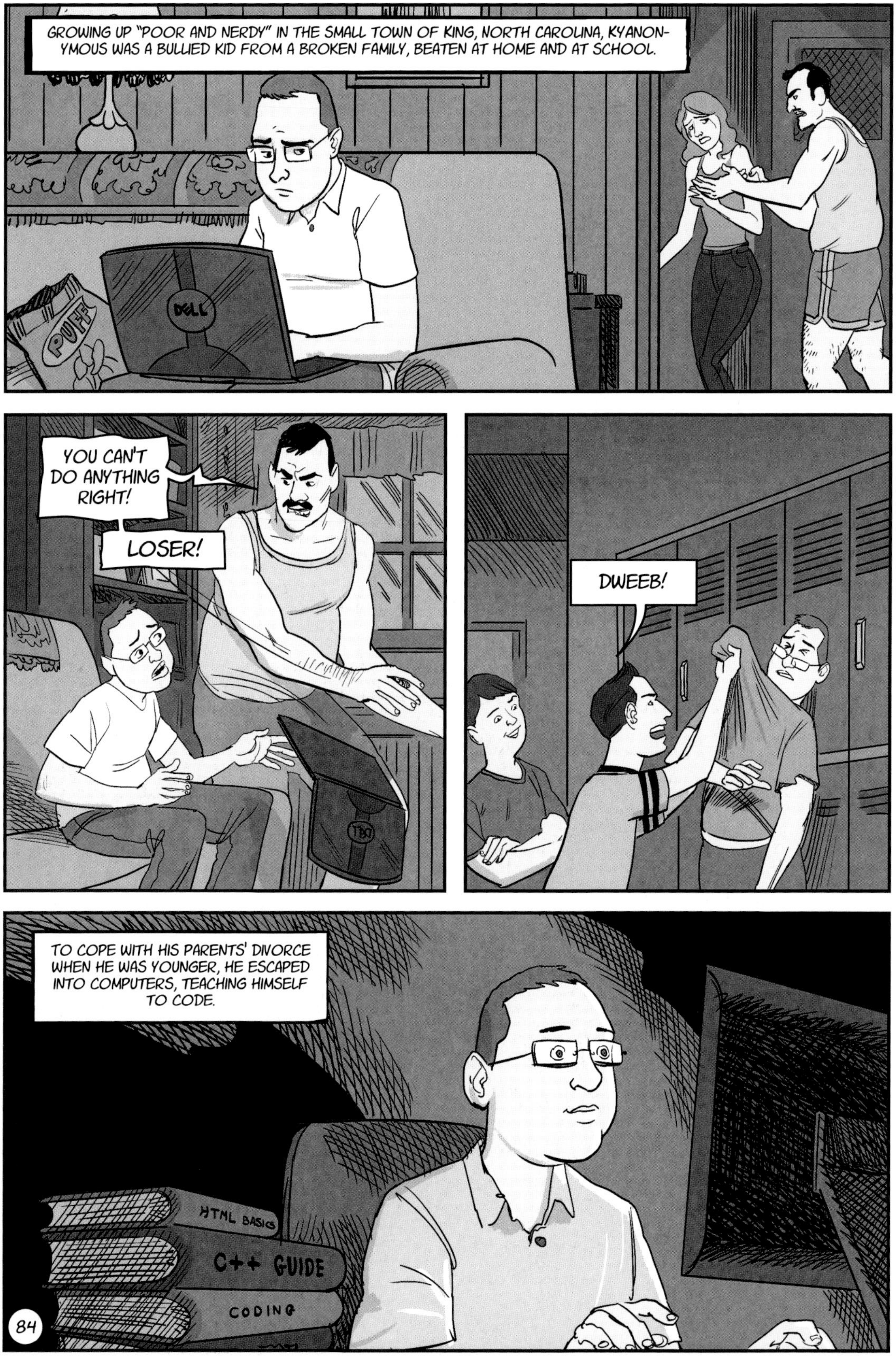
GROWING UP "POOR AND NERDY" IN THE SMALL TOWN OF KING, NORTH CAROLINA, KYANON-YMOUS WAS A BULLIED KID FROM A BROKEN FAMILY, BEATEN AT HOME AND AT SCHOOL.
DELL
PUFF
YOU CAN'T DO ANYTHING RIGHT!
LOSER!
DWEEB!
TO COPE WITH HIS PARENTS' DIVORCE WHEN HE WAS YOUNGER, HE ESCAPED INTO COMPUTERS, TEACHING HIMSELF TO CODE.
HTML BASICS
C++ GUIDE
CODING

THOUGH HE COULD BUILD HIS OWN MOTHERBOARD, HE COULDN'T HACK SCHOOL, WHERE, SCRAWNY AND SHY, HE BECAME A MORE FREQUENT TARGET.

BUT HE HAD A NASCENT VIGILANTE INSIDE HIM.

HE DECIDED TO FIGHT BACK AGAINST ANY FORM OF BULLYING.

AT SCHOOL . . .

. . . AND AT HOME, WHERE HIS MOTHER WAS BEING PHYSICALLY ABUSED BY HER BOYFRIEND.

LEAVE HER THE FUCK ALONE!

YEARS LATER, AS AN ADULT IN HIS HOMETOWN OF WINCHESTER, KENTUCKY, HIS VIGILANTE INSTINCTS DREW HIM TO ANONYMOUS.

ebay

$2.99

BUY

KY ANONYMOUS
@KYAnon

TWEETS 0   FOLLOWING 12   FOLLOWERS 1

Compose new Tweet...

86

I AM ANONYMOUS.

BUT A $2 COSTUME AND A SOCIAL NETWORK WEREN'T ENOUGH TO MAKE A DIFFERENCE IN HIS OR ANYONE ELSE'S LIFE.

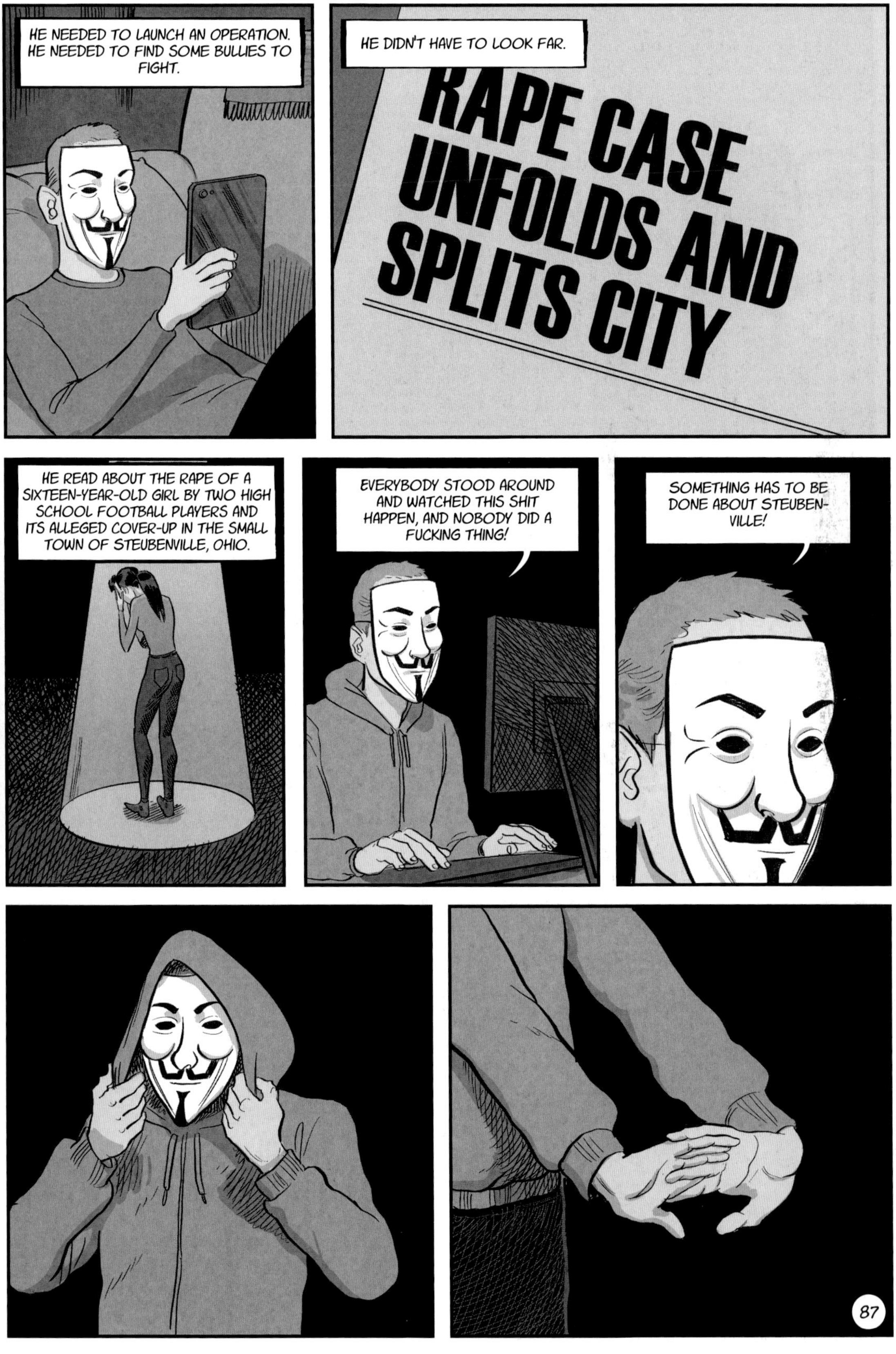
HE NEEDED TO LAUNCH AN OPERATION. HE NEEDED TO FIND SOME BULLIES TO FIGHT.
HE DIDN'T HAVE TO LOOK FAR.
RAPE CASE UNFOLDS AND SPLITS CITY
HE READ ABOUT THE RAPE OF A SIXTEEN-YEAR-OLD GIRL BY TWO HIGH SCHOOL FOOTBALL PLAYERS AND ITS ALLEGED COVER-UP IN THE SMALL TOWN OF STEUBENVILLE, OHIO.
EVERYBODY STOOD AROUND AND WATCHED THIS SHIT HAPPEN, AND NOBODY DID A FUCKING THING!
SOMETHING HAS TO BE DONE ABOUT STEUBENVILLE!

ON BEHALF OF THE VICTIM AND WITH THE SUPPORT OF CELEBRITIES, CIVILIANS, AND WELL-KNOWN ANONS, ANONYMOUS QUICKLY ORGANIZED TWO RALLIES IN STEUBENVILLE CALLED OCCUPY STEUBENVILLE.

WELCOME TO
Steubenville
A Fine Place for Home & Industry

OVER A THOUSAND PEOPLE GATHERED OUTSIDE THE COURTHOUSE IN STEUBENVILLE FOR THE PROTEST.

IN A DRAMATIC TURN, SOME OF THEM SPOKE OF THEIR OWN SEXUAL ASSAULTS AND RAPES, REMOVING THEIR MASKS TO SHOW THEMSELVES TO THE CROWD.

I TOO AM A VICTIM.

I AM A FAMILY FRIEND OF JANE DOE.

SHE SAYS SHE WAS VERY THANKFUL WE [HAD] ANONYMOUS ALONG.

SHE WAS HAPPY WE REMAINED HERE, WE WERE HER VOICE, SHE DIDN'T NEED TO SPEAK, SHE WAS AWARE OF THAT.

SHE HAS BEEN READING ALL THE TWEETS AND MESSAGES OF LOVE AND SUPPORT FROM MEMBERS OF ANONYMOUS AND THE WORLD, AND SHE IS VERY GRATEFUL.

KYANONYMOUS DIDN'T HAVE THE MONEY TO GO HIMSELF, AND FIGURED IT'D BE DANGEROUS TO DO SO ANYWAY.

AS THE CLOCK TICKED DOWN TO NEW YEAR'S EVE, THE WORLD WAS WAITING TO SEE IF THE STEUBENVILLE PLAYERS WOULD CAVE IN TO ANONYMOUS'S THREAT AND APOLOGIZE . . .

CENTER FOR SPORTS

OR FACE THE WRATH OF HAVING THEIR PERSONAL INFORMATION LEAKED ONLINE.

93

KY WASN'T SLEEPING AND WAS BARELY EATING AND INCREASINGLY PRONE TO PANIC ATTACKS.

DING!

(*_ANON

Dude, word has it that the FBI is after you.

KYANON

How do you know?

(*_ANON

I think they had an informant in Anonymous.

I'm going dark for a while.

MINUTES LATER, HE GOT A CRYPTIC MESSAGE FROM AN UNKNOWN ACCOUNT.

New Message

1

Why would you do that, Derek Lostutter of Winchester, Kentucky?

98

WHAT?!! HOW DO THEY KNOW MY REAL NAME?

ANOTHER OMINOUS MESSAGE CAME IN.

New Message

THIS ONE INCLUDED A PICTURE HE HAD PREVIOUSLY POSTED OF HIMSELF.

HE HAD TAKEN THE SHOT OUT BY THE ROAD, WHERE HE HAPPENED TO BE STANDING NEXT TO HIS BATES HOME SECURITY SIGN.

THEY KNOW WHERE I FUCKING LIVE?!

KY PANICKED.

IT WAS TIME TO SAY GOODBYE.

THE COSTUME THAT HAD PROTECTED HIM HAD BECOME A LIABILITY.

99

LOOKING AT UP TO TWENTY-FIVE YEARS IN PRISON, HE ACCEPTED A PLEA AGREEMENT, ADMITTING TO CONSPIRING TO HACK THE STEUBENVILLE HIGH SCHOOL ATHLETICS WEBSITE AND LYING TO AN FBI AGENT WHO WAS INVESTIGATING THE BREACH.

IN EXCHANGE, THE PROSECUTION DROPPED THE HACKING CHARGE UNDER THE COMPUTER FRAUD AND ABUSE ACT.

TWO YEARS IN FEDERAL PRISON!

HACKS WILL BE TAKEN SERIOUSLY AS CRIMES, NOT AS PRANKS OR PUBLICITY STUNTS.

IN STEUBENVILLE, SEVENTEEN-YEAR-OLD TRENT MAYS AND SIXTEEN-YEAR-OLD MA'LIK RICHMOND WERE CONVICTED FOR THE RAPE.

BUT THEY RECEIVED ONLY THE MINIMUM SENTENCES: ONE YEAR FOR RICHMOND, AND AN ADDITIONAL ONE FOR MAYS FOR DISTRIBUTING NUDE PICTURES OF THE VICTIM.

HALF THE TIME THAT KYANONYMOUS RECEIVED FOR TRYING TO HELP THEIR VICTIM.

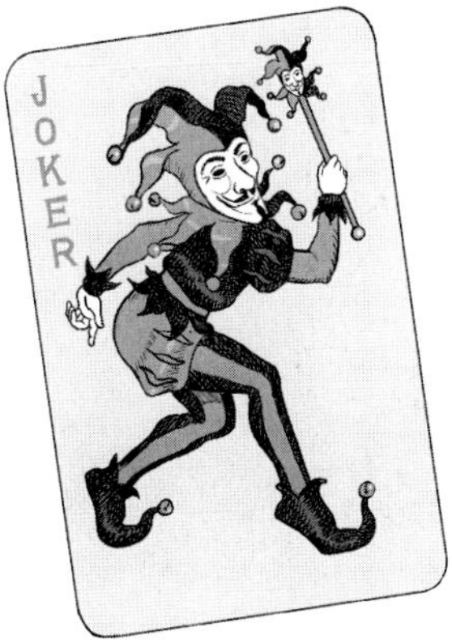
JOKER

CHAPTER 8

NOK NOK

WHAT TIME IS IT?

NINE.

IT'S HOT IN HERE!

IT'S THE SERVERS. BEEN MINING BITCOIN ALL NIGHT. IT'S A BITCH.

READY TO TALK ABOUT FERGUSON?

LET'S DO IT.

KYANONYMOUS CAME OUT OF NOWHERE, AS OPS OFTEN DO.

BUT WHAT CAME NEXT WOULD BE BIGGER--ONE OF THE HIGHEST-PROFILE ANONYMOUS OPERATIONS YET.

ON AUGUST 9, 2014, AT 5:09 P.M. LOCAL TIME, KAREEM (TEF POE) JACKSON, A RAPPER AND ACTIVIST FROM DELLWOOD, MISSOURI, A SUBURB OF ST. LOUIS, WAS WATCHING A CRISIS UNFOLDING IN A NEIGHBORING TOWN.

HE DECIDED HE HAD TO DO SOMETHING ABOUT IT.

TEF POE

Basically martial law is taking place in Ferguson. all perimeters blocked coming and going . . . National and international friends Help!!!

FIVE HOURS EARLIER IN FERGUSON, AN UNARMED EIGHTEEN-YEAR-OLD AFRICAN-AMERICAN, MICHAEL BROWN, HAD BEEN SHOT TO DEATH BY A WHITE POLICE OFFICER.

BLAM!

IN A COMMUNITY MEETING ON AUGUST 12, JON BELMAR, THE CHIEF OF THE ST. LOUIS POLICE DEPARTMENT, REFUSED.

WE DO NOT DO THAT UNTIL THEY'RE CHARGED WITH AN OFFENSE.

IN RETALIATION, A HACKER WITH THE HANDLE THEANONMESSAGE DOXED BELMAR.

Check it out! The two-hour audio file of a police radio scanner, recorded around the time of Brown's death.

Oh and here's Chief Belmar's home address, phone number, and some pix.

his son taking a snooze! now we know what he looks like.

Nice photo, Jon. Your wife actually looks good for her age. Have you had enough?

IN THE EARLY MORNING OF AUGUST 14, A FEW ANONS BECAME CONVINCED, BASED ON FACEBOOK PHOTOS AND OTHER DISPARATE CLUES, THAT BROWN'S SHOOTER WAS A THIRTY-TWO-YEAR-OLD MAN NAMED BRYAN WILLMAN.

ACCORDING TO A TRANSCRIPT OF AN IRC, ONE ANON POSTED A PHOTO OF WILLMAN WITH A SWOLLEN FACE.

THE SHOOTER CLAIMED TO HAVE BEEN HIT IN THE FACE. THIS MUST BE HIM!

I DON'T HAVE MUCH EVIDENCE ABOUT WILLMAN.

BUT I JUST CAN'T SHAKE IT. I REALLY, TRULY, HONESTLY, AND WITHOUT A SHRED OF HARD EVIDENCE THINK IT'S HIM.

FUCK IT.

3662

#RIPBryan Willman

PLEASE BE SURE. IT'S NOT JUST ABOUT A MAN'S LIFE. THE PUBLIC CAN EASILY TURN ON ANON.

6810

2411

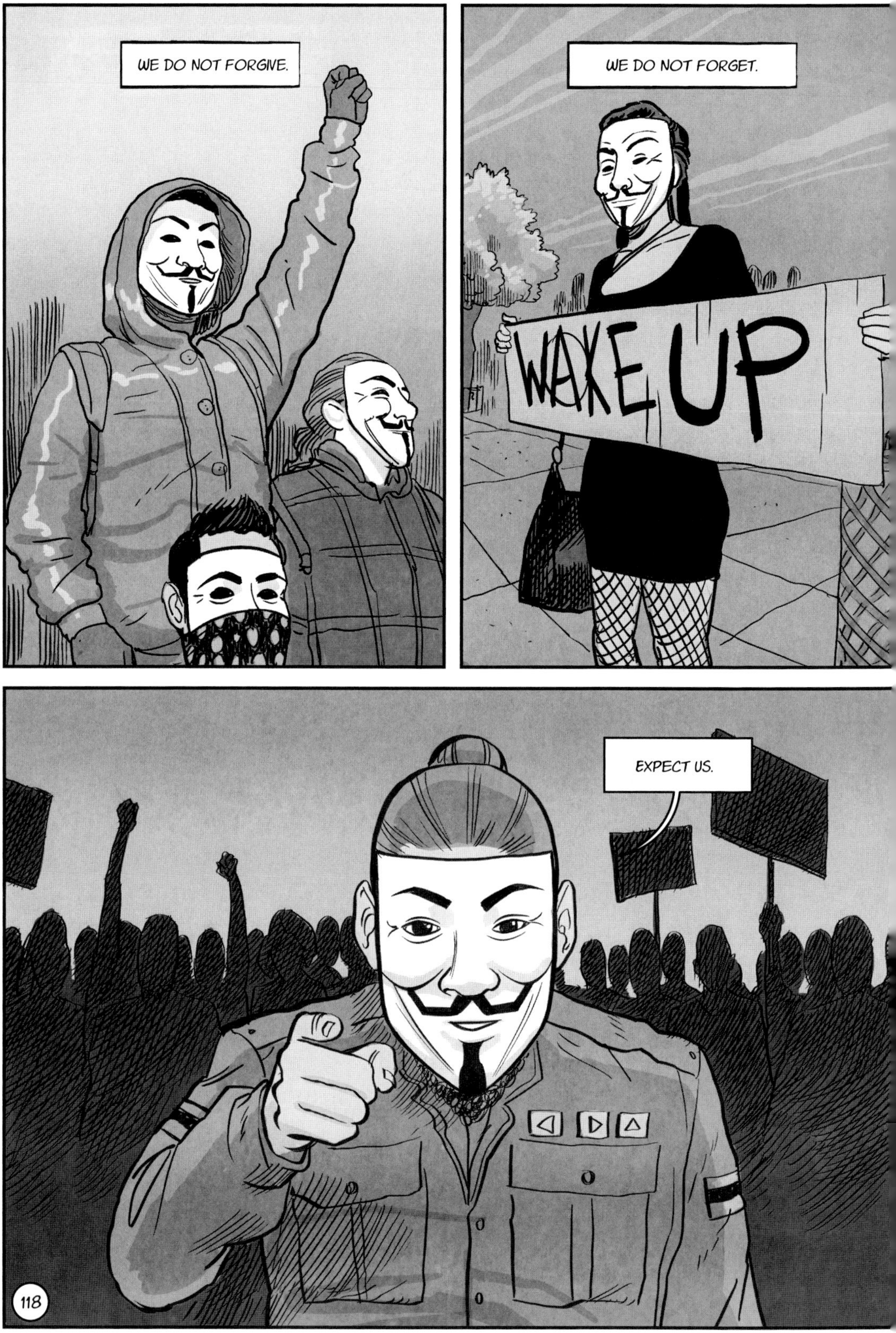
WE DO NOT FORGIVE.
WE DO NOT FORGET.
WAKE UP
EXPECT US.

GASPER TRINGALE

DAVID KUSHNER is an award-winning journalist and author. A contributing editor of *Rolling Stone* and *Outside*, Kushner has written for publications including the *New Yorker*, *Vanity Fair*, *Wired*, *New York Times Magazine*, and *GQ*. His books include *Masters of Doom*, *The Players Ball*, and *Alligator Candy*. Kushner is also author of the graphic novel *Rise of the Dungeon Master*, illustrated by Koren Shadmi.

MARY ABRAMSON

KOREN SHADMI is a Brooklyn-based illustrator and cartoonist; he studied illustration at the School of Visual Arts in NYC, where he now teaches. His graphic novels include *Rise of the Dungeon Master* and *The Twilight Man*, and his work has been published in the *New York Times*, the *New Yorker*, the *Washington Post*, *Playboy*, and *Wired*.

THE ILLUSTRATED, ~~UNTOLD STORY OF THE LEG~~ENDARY HACKTIVIST GROUP'S ORIGINS AND MOST DARING EXPLOITS

A FOR ANONYMOUS shows how a leaderless band of volunteers successfully used hacktivism to fight for the underdog and embarrass their rich and powerful targets—from Sony and PayPal to the Church of Scientology and Ferguson Police Department—all in the name of freedom of speech and information. Their exploits blurred the distinction between "online" and "reality," and helped shape our contemporary world.

DAVID KUSHNER is an award-winning journalist and author. A contributing editor of *Rolling Stone* and *Outside*, Kushner has written for the *New Yorker*, *Vanity Fair*, *Wired*, *New York Times Magazine*, and *GQ*. His books include *Masters of Doom* and *The Players Ball*. Kushner and Shadmi previously collaborated on *Rise of the Dungeon Master*.

KOREN SHADMI is a Brooklyn-based illustrator and cartoonist; he studied illustration at the School of Visual Arts in NYC, where he now teaches. His graphic novels include *Rise of the Dungeon Master* and *The Twilight Man*. His work has been published in the *New York Times*, the *New Yorker*, the *Washington Post*, *Playboy*, and *Wired*.

WE ARE ANONYMOUS

You should have expected us.

COVER DESIGN BY PETE GARCEAU | COVER ILLUSTRATIONS BY KOREN SHADMI

AVAILABLE AS AN E-BOOK

BOLD TYPE BOOKS
WWW.BOLDTYPEBOOKS.ORG

$15.99 US / $21.99 CA

ISBN-13: 978-1-56858-878-0

9 781568 588780

51599